"Richard Baxter (no, not th[illegible] offers an engaging guide to [illegible] of Catholics. Drawin[illegible] his approach [illegible] wisely encour[illegible] [illegible]uals, avoiding one-siz[illegible] theological differences such a[illegible], and justification, this book teaches u[illegible] Catholic friends with a delicate balance [illegible] grace and truth – something desperately needed in our contentious age."

Chris Castaldo, PhD, Lead Pastor, New Covenant Church, Naperville; author of *Talking with Catholics about the Gospel: A Guide for Evangelicals* and co-author of *Why Do Protestants Convert?*

"Richard Baxter's excellent book *Sharing the Gospel with a Catholic Friend* is a clear, concise, and essential resource that helpfully and charitably guides you through various key topics so you might more effectively communicate the gospel with the great variety of Catholic friends you might know or encounter. Important. Invaluable!"

Douglas Sean O'Donnell, Senior Vice President of Bible Editorial, Crossway Books

"For those of us spiritually concerned for Catholic family and friends, this insightful book primarily reminds us of the importance of seeing the person behind the label. In doing so, Richard Baxter shows us not only the basic tools we need to share our faith, but also how to use them with genuine wisdom, humility and compassion."

Jonathan Stephen, Former Provost of Union School of Theology

"With over 1.4 billion Roman Catholics worldwide, you are likely to encounter diverse perspectives on what it means to be Catholic, along with varying levels of commitment. Richard Baxter's book equips you to listen, understand, and respond appropriately. Read this book, pray, and then share the gospel with courage!"

Matt Schmucker, Director of CROSS Conference

"Richard Baxter has written a winsome and wise little book on engaging Catholics with the gospel. Catholics are people Jesus has called us to love, to whom we are called to offer Jesus as Savior. I was greatly encouraged by this work."

Ted Turnau, PhD, Chair of Arts, Culture, and Literature, Anglo-American University and author of *Popologetics*

SHARING THE GOSPEL

WITH A

CATHOLIC FRIEND

RICHARD BAXTER

10 Publishing

British Library Cataloguing in Publication Data
A record for this book is available from the British Library

ISBN: 978-1-83728-039-1

Designed and typeset by Pete Barnsley (CreativeHoot.com)

Printed in Denmark

10Publishing, a division of 10ofthose.com
6b Upper Water Street, Newry, Northern Ireland, BT34 1DJ

info@10ofthose.com
www.10ofthose.com

1 3 5 7 10 8 6 4 2

ACKNOWLEDGEMENTS

Many thanks to all who have enabled me to write this book and helped me shape both the approach I take in it and the book itself: family, churches, friends, publisher. This book isn't perfect but if it is of use, you've played a big part in that.

My greatest thanks goes to God: Father, Son and Holy Spirit. I'm far from perfect, yet in your love you have saved me and you choose to use me. One day by your grace I will be without spot or blemish, and will be with you. To you be all the glory!

CONTENTS

Introduction: My Story 1

1. Three Wrong Turns 7
2. Meet the Catholics 15
3. Considering Our Approach 23
4. Approaching the Person 29
5. Authority – Scripture and Tradition 37
6. Justification – Faith and Works 47
7. The Pope – Power and Authority 59
8. Mary – Saint and Sinner 67
9. Communion – Take and Eat 77
10. Purgatory – Death and Beyond 85

Conclusion: The Way Ahead 93

Recommended Resources 97

Endnotes 101

INTRODUCTION

MY STORY

My name is Richard Baxter, but neither my committed Catholic mum nor my atheist dad knew they were giving me the same name as the seventeenth-century Puritan who wrote *The Reformed Pastor.* Growing up in south-east England, I felt very loved by both my parents, not because of my achievements or obedience but simply because I was their son.

Throughout childhood, I went to St. Joseph's Catholic Church every Sunday evening. Though my dad was an atheist, I can't remember ever not believing in God. In fact, I believed a lot of true things about God. Most Sundays we used to say the Nicene Creed at Mass which taught me some incredibly important things. Weekly it reminded me that God the Father had created all things, that Jesus Christ is the Son of God who entered our world, and that he lived, died and amazingly rose again from death.

As a child I found church services boring, and they signalled the end of the weekend. However, around the age of fourteen, when many young people stopped attending church, I began to take my faith more seriously. I was confirmed and started to enjoy going to Mass. I was an altar server up until my late teens – one time serving for the Bishop of the Diocese of Arundel and Brighton, Cormac Murphy O'Connor, who later became a Cardinal of the Catholic Church.

As a baptised Catholic looking to take my faith seriously, I was aware I sometimes still did wrong things. But here was my thinking: even though I sinned, if I did *this, this* and *this* good thing, then God would hopefully love me, forgive me and accept me into heaven.

Going away to university in West Wales, I continued to go to Mass every weekend. I also went to the university's Christian Union meetings – after all, I considered myself a

Christian, so there was no reason I wouldn't! The people at the CU were a little odd; I noticed that they didn't get drunk or swear. They were very nice and welcoming though, and I liked going.

One Friday evening meeting I didn't enjoy, however. The speaker that night grew up as a Catholic in Northern Ireland, had been injured while building a bomb for a paramilitary group, and then became a Protestant through reading the Bible while in hospital.

Growing up in the UK in the 1980s and 1990s, my frame of reference for "Catholic" and "Protestant" was the Troubles in Northern Ireland, where it seemed the conflict between the groups had little to do with theological differences. However, as this man spoke, he told us repeatedly, "The Catholic Church teaches X but the Bible says Y."

I was very angry to begin with, recognising that he was calling my Christian faith into question; something that had never happened to me before. By the end of the evening, however, my anger had given way to upset and confusion. How could I know if what he was saying was true? Despite being a keen reader, I had never read more than a couple of pages of the Bible myself. The Lord in his grace brought over a friend who I had spoken to once or twice before; I told him how I was feeling and he offered to read John's Gospel with me.

In the months following, Jonathan and I met together every week to look at John's Gospel. I began by trying to work out everything the Catholic Church teaches, everything other churches teach, and deciding which is right. After a few weeks I realised I wasn't clever enough to do this, and so instead started to really listen to the words of Jesus; something which Jonathan had wanted us to be doing from the beginning!

As I did so, I began to realise that my plan to do good things to get to God was a non-starter; Jesus says that everyone who sins is a slave to sin – we can't stop serving it. I began to realise sin's heaviness: it isn't just a small thing to overcome but something that separates us from God. However, I also began to see that though I cannot reach up to God, he has still loved me and reached down to raise me up. Despite remaining conflicted over some issues, I realised why the Father had sent Jesus: to live the life I had failed to live, to die the death I deserved, and to rise again to give me new life.

One afternoon in tears I told my friend that I now knew I wasn't right with God, but I wasn't sure how to change this. He asked if I had prayed about it and I had to admit I hadn't! As I walked to my room that evening I prayed, asking if God was the one I had been reading about in John's Gospel, he would let me know. I felt an immediate, overwhelming sense of peace wash over me, and it was then that I trusted in Jesus and gave my life over to him.

I discovered, and am continuing to realise now, that God is far more like a loving parent than I had assumed; that though he hates sin, I didn't need to earn his favour. He loved me, and sent his Son to save me. I didn't need to bring myself back to God; Jesus is the one who brings us to God. It was that freeness of the gospel that excited me then, and which still amazes me almost thirty years later.

1
THREE WRONG TURNS

The Apostle Paul says, "I could wish that I myself were cursed and cut off from Christ for the sake of my people, those of my own race, the people of Israel" (Rom. 9:3-4). Paul's desire to see his own people come to know the Lord is so great, he would be willingly cut off from salvation, in order that they might be saved.

I don't think I can claim my feelings for "my people" are as strong as Paul's. However, I really desire to see Catholics coming to know God's full, free salvation through Jesus, having the comfort of the gospel, and glorifying God as they live in the power of the Spirit.

Given that there are around 1.4 billion baptised Catholics alive today, this is a subject that should be important to all Christians. I'm so glad you've picked up this book, even if you're simply reading it in the bookshop without paying for it. I hope you find something helpful before an assistant asks you to buy it or put it down.

But as we begin, it's worth asking, aren't Catholics already Christians? You may feel uncomfortable talking about sharing the gospel with people who already worship Jesus. Or alternatively, should we assume instead every Catholic is without true faith and therefore dead in their sins? Maybe you feel that we should approach them as we would any other non-Christian.

There are various wrong turns to avoid as we think through engaging with our Catholic friends – but what are they?

TO CONSIDER:

Before going further, please take a few moments to note down some answers to these two questions:

CONTINUE ↓

What Catholics do you know?

What do you know about Catholic teaching?

Reflecting on what, and who, you know will be really helpful as we consider sharing the gospel with our specific friends. We'll come back to your answers in chapter 3.

WRONG TURN ONE: IT'S ALL BAD

When thinking about the gospel and our Catholic friends, we can make a few wrong turns. The first common mistake is to think that nothing the Catholic Church teaches is true or good. From the outside looking in we may see a greater emphasis on Mary than on Jesus, along with people hoping their goodness will get them to heaven and church structures that look very different to those described in the New Testament, and conclude everything about its teaching is totally wrong. That's simply not the case.

Looking back, I'm genuinely so thankful for aspects of my Catholic upbringing. Because we said the creeds regularly on Sundays, I really understood that there is one God in three Persons; Father, Son and Holy Spirit. I knew that Jesus Christ is both God and man, that he had died and risen again.

Every Sunday I would hear readings from a psalm, another Old Testament passage, a New Testament letter, and the Gospels. That's more of God's Word read aloud each week than in most evangelical church services.

There was also so much in terms of ethics and morals that was good and true. Things I was taught about marriage and sexuality for example were completely biblical. Culture has obviously shifted a lot since I was growing up in the eighties and nineties but even then, there would have been things I might have been confused about without the teaching I received.

The Catholic Church also has a genuine concern for the vulnerable, both for the born and for the unborn. We shouldn't forget these common beliefs and values when we are seeking to share the gospel with our Catholic friends.

But then there's …

WRONG TURN TWO: IT'S ALL GOOD

A second mistake is to imagine that the differences between Catholic and evangelical beliefs are small and unimportant. But there exist big, important differences – not just based on church traditions and preferences – that are central to the good news of Jesus.

Growing up, I knew Jesus had died and risen again. I even wore a crucifix around my neck for years to remind me of that truth. However, though I believed in the reality of those events, I had no idea about their purpose until I began to read John's Gospel for myself at university.

GOOD TO KNOW:

Official Roman Catholic teaching does recognise Jesus as the sacrifice for sin and that we are not simply saved by our good works, though many baptised Catholics remain confused on this point as Peter Kreeft explains:

> "There are still many who do not know … the gospel. Most of my Catholic students … do not even know how to get to heaven. When I ask them what they would say to God if they died tonight and God asked them why he should take them into heaven, nine out of ten do not even mention Jesus Christ. Most of them say they have been good or kind or sincere or did their best."[1]

Kreeft, himself a faithful Roman Catholic, recognises the need for Catholics to hear and understand about God's saving grace in Jesus.

CONTINUE ↓

> We won't want to argue with that, and we'll want to help our Catholic friends hear that message of God's grace!

Though my understanding of salvation did not accurately reflect official Catholic teaching, it probably reflects the beliefs of many of the Catholics you meet. However, there are also big problems with the official Catholic understanding of how the sacrifice of Jesus works, and particularly how we receive the benefits of it. There are many other important differences too and some of these will be covered in more detail in the second half of the book.

Then there's …

WRONG TURN THREE: THEY'RE ALL THE SAME

We can imagine that when someone says, "I'm Catholic", they're telling us a lot about what they actually believe. But with about 1.4 billion Catholics in the world, it seems unlikely they will all believe the same things.

In the next chapter, I'll introduce you to five types of Catholics you might meet. This is not necessarily an exhaustive list, however, as you read these descriptions, I hope it might help you understand where different friends are coming from. Perhaps you'll also be able to think about how they match up with people from other faith and non-faith backgrounds too. More importantly, I hope it will help as you consider how to share the good news of Jesus with specific individuals.

2

MEET THE CATHOLICS

Imagine a Catholic. What type of person comes into your mind? An elderly lady with a string of Rosary beads? A stern-looking man with an unusually tall hat? A young person who is indistinguishable from others around them, except that they claim the name "Catholic"? A Christian believer exuding warmth and love for Christ? As you read this chapter, I hope what will be clear is that Catholics – and our Catholic friends – come in as many shapes and sizes as the rest of us!

DOCTRINAL DANNY AND DOCTRINAL DANIELLE

Let me introduce you to two siblings who really understand – and believe – official Roman Catholic doctrine.

First there's Danny, the older brother. He believes in the statements made at the Catholic Council of Trent in the sixteenth century and much that followed from that. Trent's teachings were in many ways a response to the Protestant Reformation, and a rejection of what Reformers like Martin Luther taught. Danny is quite suspicious of Protestants or evangelicals, though he may or may not know what we actually believe.

It seems that people who have moved in their faith commitment from evangelical to Catholic often fall into the Doctrinal Danny category. They may feel the Roman Catholic Church is more historically rooted, more stable, more majestic than their evangelical upbringing, and this is attractive to them.

GOOD TO KNOW:

A council is simply a meeting of church leaders who get together to discuss and make decisions about church teaching. This is neither good or bad in itself; the Jerusalem Council in Acts 15 made great decisions, as have many other councils through the church's history. It really depends on whether what is decided agrees with what God says in the Scriptures!

Then there's Danny's younger sister Doctrinal Danielle, who is much more into the official Catholic teachings as formulated at the Second Vatican Council (Vatican II) in the 1960s. These teachings, and much that has followed, were self-consciously updating Catholic teaching. While they might look quite different to us from what went before (for example, there now seems far more openness to the possibility of salvation for those outside the Roman Catholic Church than previously), the Catholic Church sees no opposition between Vatican II and Trent. Danielle may well be much more open than her brother to friendly dialogue with you and to finding common ground – as well as with people from other religions.

Both Danny and Danielle can say they believe in official Catholic teaching, and yet both can have very different emphases in what they believe – and at least to us it might seem they believe some contradictory things.

CONFUSED CONNOR

Next meet Connor. This was definitely me before I came to know the Lord. Confused Connor believes in God. In fact, he might well consider himself to have a personal faith, but he probably won't know what the Bible says about lots of things or what the official teachings of the Catholic Church are. Connor might have all kinds of views that aren't in line with official Catholic doctrine and ethics. However, even though he is confused about the gospel and how he can know God's forgiveness, he has some kind of belief which is important to him.

INDIFFERENT INGRID

Then there's Ingrid who perhaps grew up in a predominantly Catholic country. Though she goes to Mass no more than once or twice a year if that, and doesn't really think about how Christian faith should impact daily living, she is one hundred per cent Catholic – nobody should dare suggest otherwise.

For other Ingrids, the externals of the religion are so tied in to their culture or upbringing that they'll do a lot more than just tick the box in a census. They willingly conform to the outward rhythms of the Catholic life, but as for personal faith, it is not really there.

TO CONSIDER:

I knew an atheist who, when the Jehovah's Witnesses would knock on the door, would tell them "Sorry, we're Catholic" – falling to mention that it was his wife, rather than himself, who was Catholic. He wasn't telling them anything about what he did or didn't believe but was instead short-circuiting a conversation about faith, because he wasn't interested in having one with them.

Though many Ingrids are not actively unbelieving in this way, they may use the label

CONTINUE ↓

"Catholic" as a way to deter religious debates rather than as a positive statement of faith. Will they be interested in a Catholic/Protestant debate? It seems unlikely. But they are still someone who needs to hear the good news of Jesus, and so we will want to pray for them, and look for opportunities to speak to them.

BORN-AGAIN BOBBY

Born-Again Bobby's name speaks for itself, doesn't it? Bobby really does trust in Jesus Christ, knowing that the Son of God loved her and gave himself for her. Bobby doesn't rely on her goodness, but on the grace of God shown towards her in the Lord Jesus Christ. She quite probably believes things that I don't. She might well believe some things that seem to me to be quite problematic. She likely thinks there are things that evangelicals believe that are unbiblical. But she is a believer; a sister in the Lord Jesus.

Hopefully this chapter has shown or reminded you that to simply imagine a generic Catholic is impossible. The 1.4 billion Catholics in the world are as diverse – not only in background, age and ethnicity, but even in what they believe and hold dear – as any other group of people spread across the planet. It is far more possible, and far more important, to consider how to share the gospel with a specific Catholic friend. That's what we'll begin to do in the next chapter.

3
CONSIDERING OUR APPROACH

Recently I chatted with a young Catholic and, over the course of a forty-minute conversation, there were times when he was a Doctrinal Danny, times when he really seemed to be a Born-Again Bobby, and times when he appeared to be a Confused Connor.

The categories in the previous chapter aren't meant to be vacuum sealed, as though a person only ever fits into one of them. They are simply to point out that when someone says to you "I'm Catholic", it isn't necessarily telling you much about what they believe.

They might be an Ingrid, trying to avoid talking about religion. Perhaps they're a Connor who believes we must do good things to be saved. Maybe they're a Bobby who wants to rejoice in Christ's salvation along with you. We shouldn't seek to share the gospel in the exact same way to each one.

NOT ALL CATHOLICS ARE DANNYS

Quite often we treat everyone that calls themselves a Catholic as though they are a Doctrinal Danny or Danielle. That's certainly what happened to me. The very first time I went to an evangelical church, I was introduced to someone in the coffee time after the service. I told him, "I'm Catholic, but I'm exploring what other Christians believe."

He immediately responded, "There are seven major problems with the doctrine of the Roman Catholic Church", and he went on to tell me what those problems were for the next several minutes. What he said was probably accurate, but I can't be sure because my eyes had glazed over within the first ten seconds. Having assumed I was a Doctrinal Danny, he launched into what he thought was a great "gospel" presentation for any Catholic. But I had no idea what he was talking about!

Many books on Roman Catholicism from an evangelical perspective address the convinced Danny or Danielle. While it is good for us to be informed about official Catholic teaching, unless you spend all your time in YouTube comment sections, Danny and Danielle will probably be a minority of Catholics you meet. (Do check out the recommended resources section at the back of this book if you are seeking to share the gospel with a well-informed Catholic.) However, whichever category a Catholic friend falls into, a positive knowledge of the gospel, love for the person, and prayerful reliance on God will always be more helpful than an in-depth knowledge of Catholic doctrine.

CONSIDER THE INDIVIDUAL

Back to those names you wrote down in chapter 1. Do the individuals you know believe the aspects of Catholic teaching you jotted down? It's good to find out because if we assume Indifferent Ingrid thinks some church traditions are as authoritative as the Bible, and you start explaining why that isn't the case, she probably isn't going to care. Ingrid doesn't view either Sacred Tradition or Sacred Scripture as her authority.

If we assume Confused Connor believes we are justified by infused rather than imputed righteousness and we launch into a conversation about that, we're likely to leave him entirely bewildered – like I've perhaps just left you by using those terms!

If we tell Doctrinal Danny that he shouldn't worship Mary, he'll rightly tell us that Catholic teaching agrees with us. He may also think we aren't worth engaging with, because we don't understand the teaching we're trying to push back against.

And what if we accuse Born-Again Bobby of believing we get to God by our good works, when she's actually trusting entirely in what Christ has done for her? Well, we could miss out on an encouraging conversation and perhaps lose an opportunity to gently show her that the type of churches we go to and the approach we take to God's Word could be helpful for her walk with Jesus too.

If we miss the fact we're talking to an individual, we probably will fail to connect well with our friend. So I would encourage you to try and get to know them and what they believe and not assume you already know!

TO CONSIDER:

When sharing the gospel with a Catholic friend, rather than asserting what we think we know, I'd suggest you to do three things in particular:

- Ask questions.
- Share your story of God's grace in your life.
- Share Scripture.

Asking questions is great because you really want to know what your friend believes and how you can speak the gospel to them in a way that they will understand and see the relevance of.

When we share our story, we're using the gift God has given to us personally in order to bless someone else. Also, since we are considering

CONTINUE ↓

sharing the good news with friends, hopefully they have a natural care for and interest in us, just as we do with them.

When we open up the Bible together, we are on common ground as Scripture is an authority for both us and our friend. Not only that, as God's Word goes forth (from an armchair as well as from the pulpit), it has spiritual power to bring light, life and faith in the Lord Jesus.

Later in this book, we will look briefly at some different areas of Catholic teaching and how we might address them. We'll think about how to share something of the gospel with a Catholic friend in relation to each topic. However, since not everyone is a Danny, you may never discuss some – or even most – of these specific issues with a Catholic, and yet still faithfully share the gospel with them.

4

APPROACHING THE PERSON

Imagine you've just been introduced to a friend of a friend who mentions they are Catholic. Is your task to quickly categorise the person and then drop one of five pre-packaged gospel presentations on them? No! Whether we find ourselves talking to a Danny or Danielle, Connor, Ingrid or Bobby, or someone who seems to be switching between the different positions, there is one thing to remember above everything else: God genuinely wants this person, made in his image, to know him through Jesus his Son.

Because God genuinely wants them to know him, so do we. Because they are precious to God, they must be precious to us. So let's consider briefly how our approach to sharing the gospel with each might look.

DOCTRINAL DANNY AND DANIELLE

Surely you can at least rely on Danny and Danielle to believe official Catholic doctrine and so, having found common ground in ethics, you can simply get on with telling them what's wrong with Catholicism, right?

Three cautions: First, they will know far more about Catholic doctrine and Catholic practice than you do. If you jump in with accusations, you may find that what appeared so clear in the book you read comes out as a garbled mess. So, rather than making a statement, ask questions to clarify what they actually believe, and continue to ask questions about what Scripture teaches on an issue.

Second, they may well have assumptions about what evangelicals teach, so be prepared to gently counter a wrong understanding of what you believe and to patiently explain your beliefs from the Bible.

Third, you need to ask: Am I really more interested in telling Danny and Danielle what is wrong with Catholicism than in pointing them to the truth, goodness, and beauty of Christ and his full salvation? Surely not. Let's talk about Jesus!

CONFUSED CONNOR

Who knows what Connor does and doesn't believe – unless you ask him? I'd encourage you to ask questions about his beliefs about Jesus and salvation *and* to positively share the basics of the gospel with him.

I'd also suggest you don't bother trying to discuss specific Catholic teachings, unless Connor himself raises them. Though I was a Catholic I didn't believe the Pope was infallible and so raising this issue with me really was a Red Herring. Why waste time explaining and debating something neither of you believe? But you can be sure he needs to hear about Jesus Christ dying for sin and rising to give us life – full, free and forever.

INDIFFERENT INGRID

We might feel tempted to leave Indifferent Ingrid to her cultural Catholicism that doesn't go much beyond a tick on a census and a visit to Midnight Mass on Christmas Eve. After all, it can seem hard to move forward in conversation with someone who isn't very interested in her own faith, let alone ours!

But we believe that her life and eternity would be transformed by knowing Jesus, so we need to try. Let's ask questions to find out what makes Ingrid tick and be genuinely interested to find out. Then as we get the opportunity, gently try to help her see, as Saint Paul tells the people in Lystra, "[God] has shown kindness by giving you rain from heaven and crops in their seasons; he provides you with plenty of food and fills your heart with joy" (Acts 14:17).

Everything Ingrid values finds its foundation in the God and Father of our Lord Jesus Christ. Every good thing she enjoys comes down as a gift from the Father of lights. And the Lord is calling Ingrid to turn away from idolatry, and turn to him – the living, powerful, joy-giving God.

TO CONSIDER:

You may notice at times I use the term "Saint" to refer to specific believers such as Peter, Paul and others. This is something Catholics do, and it can sound strange to them when evangelicals don't. Of course, we may want to point out that every believer is truly a saint – the greetings of many of the New Testament letters indicate this clearly – rather than only believers in biblical times and church history. However, surely we can ***also*** refer to the believers of old as saints, especially if it will help our Catholic friend to listen well to what we are saying!

BORN-AGAIN BOBBY

How about Born-Again Bobby? Well, share with her as you would another Christian brother or sister. Of course, you recognise that a Roman Catholic Church isn't going to be the best place for your friend to grow. But if all you do is tell her that, she probably won't want to talk about faith with you – just like you probably don't really want to chat with that friend who spends the whole time telling you how naughty your children are or how messy your house is.

And you don't *only* want her to start going to a church where the gospel is taught with greater clarity; you actually do want her to grow in her faith. So, talk to her about what you've been reading in God's Word – encourage her with what you've been learning about Christ. Of course, as contentious issues come up, discuss them openly and honestly, assuring her of your love and friendship even in disagreement. Ask questions such as, "Can I ask why you believe that?" or "Does the Bible teach that anywhere?"

And if it turns out that Born-Again Bobby isn't actually born again? Well, she's heard a bunch of truth about God and his Son – and that has to be a good thing!

TO CONSIDER:

As we talk about the gospel with our Catholic friends – whether that's Doctrinal Danny and Danielle, Confused Connor, Indifferent Ingrid or Born-Again Bobby – there is a time for challenge. That preacher at the Christian Union

CONTINUE ↓

certainly challenged me, and this formed part of my journey of coming to know the Lord. But do what you can to make it a challenge that will actually hit home because it relates to what your friend actually believes, rather than what they don't. Otherwise, you're likely to either cause needless offence, or like me on my first visit to an evangelical church, your friend's eyes may quickly glaze over.

5

AUTHORITY

SCRIPTURE AND TRADITION

TO CONSIDER:

Hey there reader. It's possible you've jumped straight to this chapter, as it is the first to deal with a specific subject on which Catholic and evangelical teaching disagree. I can't stop you doing that! But the main focus here is on sharing the good news of Jesus with a *particular* Catholic friend rather than a comprehensive comparison of doctrine. I promise the first few chapters won't take long to read and the rest of the book will be a lot more helpful after reading them. Hopefully see you back here in twenty minutes!

WE CAN UNDERSTAND THE BIBLE!

Evangelical Christians believe the Scriptures to be the sole, infallible source of authority for Christian faith and practice. In other words, if we want to be certain what God says on a specific subject, we turn to the Bible. This way of understanding revelation is often called *Sola Scriptura*. In this view, we see ourselves as direct descendants of the sixteenth-century Protestants who sought to reform the church's faith and worship according to God's Word.

Official Catholic teaching, on the other hand, tells us that the church "does not derive her certainty about all revealed truths from the holy Scriptures alone. Both Scripture and Tradition must be accepted and honoured with equal sentiments of devotion and reverence."[1] In other words, if we are to know what God has said, looking to the Bible is not enough; we must also consider what tradition teaches.

GOOD TO KNOW:

Not every tradition is infallible according to Catholic teaching. It is only Sacred Tradition

CONTINUE ↓

which holds this authority. So, how do Catholics know what that Sacred Tradition is and how to understand it? Ultimately, they are taught to listen to the church, which the Holy Spirit guides. It is the Magisterium – the teaching council of the Roman Catholic Church – that has the authority to interpret *both* Scripture *and* Tradition.

You probably recognise that putting tradition on an equal standing with the Bible gives too much authority to a fallible institution (the church), and can take away the impetus for people to read and understand the Bible for themselves. I remember once offering a Gospel to a friend who sometimes went to the Catholic Church I grew up in. His reply remains with me, "Father Bill tells me what I need to know." In his mind, he didn't need to read about the life, death and resurrection of Jesus Christ because a priest, on behalf of the church, would tell him all he needed to know. Likewise, many of our Catholic friends may well believe they cannot understand God's Word without someone else interpreting it for them so don't even consider studying it for themselves.

SEEING OUR OWN PITFALLS

There is of course a danger that we swing too far the other way and have a "just me and my Bible" approach to the Christian faith. We can neglect fellowship and learning from other believers, proudly thinking that our own understanding of any given Scripture will of course be the correct one. This would also be wrong! God has gifted his church with Bible teachers to help us understand his Word, and we would be foolish to ignore the ways God's Spirit has guided his church over the last 2,000 years. Rightly understood, the evangelical view of *Sola Scriptura* is a helpful safeguard. It does not neglect tradition and theological thinking, but causes them to be submitted to what Scripture itself says.

Unity is very important in Catholicism, and your friend may think the reason for so much disunity in Protestantism is *Sola Scriptura.* They may conclude that, with no Magisterium – no central authority – to tell us what to believe, as soon as we disagree on the meaning of the Bible, we break off and start a new church!

To help counter this caricature, you could *talk* with them about how there is unity amongst evangelical churches on what Saint Paul calls the "things of first importance": Christ's death for our sin and his true rising again (1 Cor. 15:3-8). Of course, some churches deny these things of first importance, but that is not through a different reading of Scripture but a denial of it. You should also be able to *show* your friend this unity through gospel churches working together and Christians from different churches loving one another as brothers and sisters.

WHAT ARE YOU AIMING AT?

The concept that Scripture cannot be understood by the individual believer seems to be at odds with the Bible itself. We are told in the Old Testament, "Your word is a lamp for my feet, a light for my path" (Ps. 119:105). God's Word gives light to us, so that we can understand him, the world around us, and ourselves. But how can we help our friend see this?

One way of "helping" a Catholic friend consider where we find ultimate authority would be to try and prove to them that the Bible outranks Sacred Tradition. To do this, you could debate the nature and history of tradition in the teaching of the Christian church, with you citing your apologists and them citing theirs. This is likely to lead to a stalemate.

Alternatively, you could show them the wonderful goodness of the Bible, and that they *can* understand what God says there for themselves. This might not immediately cause them to accept *Sola Scriptura*, but it may help them recognise that God truly is speaking to them in the Bible.

TO CONSIDER:

"Oh, you're Catholic. You're not allowed to read the Bible, are you?" Hopefully you can see for both Confused Connor and Born-Again Bobby, this question is pretty accusatory and off-putting. And Doctrinal Danielle knows it simply isn't true. Catholics *are* allowed to read the Bible. Whatever the history of this issue might be, your friend lives in the twenty-first century, not the sixteenth!

Whether they read it or not, most Catholics will own a Bible, and a great thing about sharing Scripture with a Catholic friend is that Catholic

CONTINUE ↓

translations of the Bible (such as the New Jerusalem Bible) are generally speaking helpful translations. If you think your friend might be suspicious of a "Protestant" Bible, you should feel free to share biblical truth from their own Bible with them.

YOU COULD TRY

You could ask your friend if they have a favourite Bible passage or story. Because long chunks of Scripture are read at Mass, Catholics are more likely to know a story than a "memory verse". Surely, whatever their favourite story or verse is, we can talk about the gospel from that. And perhaps they'll ask us for ours, and we can share something of the gospel again!

Of course, Indifferent Ingrid probably doesn't have a favourite Bible story. She might not be interested in gaining one either. She doesn't see either Scripture or tradition as having much authority. Could you share a Bible verse which she can see is really helpful practical advice?

I might try Proverbs 15:1, "A gentle answer turns away wrath, but a harsh word stirs up anger" and a couple of sentences about how this changed the way I work with teenagers. Or maybe she is one of many people who has no interest in the Bible but claims a high respect for Jesus. If so, she might be open to hearing a story about Jesus' welcome of outsiders (e.g. Luke 7:36-50) that will convince her that here is a man who is worth listening to.

Since many Catholics feel intimidated at the idea of reading the Bible for themselves, any opportunity to look at the Bible with your friend, even when you're reading things you both agree on, is a victory. It is in the Scriptures, more than anywhere else, that they will encounter Jesus the Saviour – and so will you as you read the Bible with them!

GOOD TO KNOW:

You may know that the Roman Catholic canon of Scripture is longer than the sixty-six books Protestants have in their Bibles. This is because extra books (or sections of books) not in the Jewish (Hebrew) canon of Scripture were included in the Greek translation of the Old

CONTINUE ↓

Testament called the Septuagint and these are kept in Catholic Bibles today.

Protestants do not view these works as part of of sacred Scripture, though many recognise they can, like many other books, be both helpful and beautiful. Protestants usually call these books the "Apocrypha", a word that has often come to mean "of doubtful authenticity". You can imagine that a Catholic who values these books won't be keen on them being called that! They generally prefer the term "Deuterocanon" – a second canon. Indeed, they won't consider them as books that the Catholic Church has added; rather an informed Catholic would suggest that Protestants removed them.

This is a historically complex topic. For example, while the Early Church Fathers considered them helpful, some – such as St. Jerome – did not value these books as highly as Scripture. Others – including Augustine of Hippo – accepted them as God's Word.

Rather than try and debate your Catholic friend, if your conversation turns to these books, why not ask, "Do you have a favourite part of the Deuterocanon?" If they don't, and if they

CONTINUE

haven't even read it, is it really worth having a debate over its usefulness?

If your friend does place great value on the Deuterocanon, you could say, "Jesus said that all the Scriptures speak about him in John 5:39. What parts of those books do you really love for how they show you who he is and what he came to do?" This will take the conversation back to the Word of God – Jesus – the one God's written Word points to.

6

JUSTIFICATION

FAITH AND WORKS

In the UK, local newspapers have a reputation for getting information wrong. Although this is frustrating for those directly involved, whether Sharon Sullivan was forty-six or forty-nine years old, and whether her car was stolen in Middle Wallop or Nether Wallop will not be relevant to most readers.

The subject of this chapter is one that is very easy to get wrong. Protestants can (and do) easily misunderstand, and therefore misrepresent, Catholic teaching on justification. This is especially so since the emphasis in Catholic teaching seems to have changed in recent centuries, so our doctrinally aware friends Danny and Danielle may sound quite different from each other when they're talking about the subject. But despite the challenges, the issue of how we are made right with God is vitally relevant to us all, so it is important to try to get the details correct.

Justification was a key issue in the Protestant Reformation of the sixteenth century, and remains central today. As you read the rest of this book, you'll hopefully recognise that specific Roman Catholic doctrines diverge from evangelical doctrine largely because of different views of justification (as well as of Scripture's unique authority). So, as technical as this chapter may seem at times, it is an important one theologically. It's also important to us as individuals – though it can be hard to understand and distinguish different views, right understanding of this truth brings assurance and joy to us, and to our Catholic friends.

GOOD TO KNOW:

The word "Justification" can seem daunting but it simply means to be made right with God. The

CONTINUE ↓

big question is, how can we – sinners – be made right with him?

According to the Apostle Paul in Romans 3:21-24, God the Judge declares a sinner "Not Guilty" when they put their faith in Jesus. They are now "justified" and God views them as completely righteous in his sight. This happens not because of what they have done (their works) but because they are joined to Jesus Christ, the utterly Righteous One. In line with Paul's teaching, evangelicals believe justification is not achieved by our good works in any way, but happens because of God's freely given, unearned love (his grace).

MORE THAN FAITH?

As I mentioned earlier, the widespread belief we are simply saved by our good works does not actually represent official Catholic teaching. In fact, the sixteenth-century Council of Trent declares, "If any one saith, that man may be justified before God by his own works, whether done through the teaching of human nature, or that of the law, without the grace of God through Jesus Christ; let him be anathema [cut off from the Catholic Church]."[1]

Though many Catholics – including me when I was growing up – don't realise it, Catholic teaching says we must rely on God's grace if we are to be in a right relationship with him. The Catholic Church is clear that we cannot be justified before God apart from his grace shown to us in Jesus Christ.

However, though God's grace is vital, it isn't the full picture according to Roman Catholic theology. While we are justified in the first place only by God's grace, not good deeds, Catholic teaching tells us that by the Holy Spirit's help "we can merit for ourselves and for others all the graces needed to attain eternal life".[2] To receive eternal life with God, we must *work towards* the grace we need in order to receive it. Though even the believer's good works are enabled by grace, in Catholic teaching *our* good works are an essential part of our salvation. To put it another way, while initial justification is by grace alone, we must grow in that justification, and our grace-enabled works bring that growth.

GOOD TO KNOW:

Though it may seem similar in many ways, the official Roman Catholic teaching is not the gospel the Scriptures teach. The good news is that we are justified from start to finish all through the grace which comes through faith in the Lord Jesus Christ and what he has achieved on our behalf. Since our works don't contribute to our salvation in any way, justification is not a process as the Catholic Church teaches.

God declares us righteous the moment we become a Christian because we are joined to Jesus the Righteous One through trust in him. Sadly, this biblical gospel has been condemned by the same Council of Trent which I quoted earlier, saying that we must not claim to be justified by faith alone, and that if we do so we are cut off from the Catholic Church.[3]

As with all the doctrines we discuss, it's quite possible that most Catholics you meet won't necessarily hold to or be able to articulate the official Catholic view of justification. Some Born-Again Bobbys will have a more biblical understanding of God's grace. Many Confused Connors will believe what I did – that we simply work our way to God by our good actions. Indifferent Ingrid, of course, will view all this as largely irrelevant to her daily life – but will probably subconsciously think being good is good enough. Below, we will think about how we might open a conversation with our Catholic friends on this important issue.

TO CONSIDER:

Why do many Catholics seem to struggle so much with the idea of justification by grace alone, through faith alone, in Christ alone?

Firstly, all of us naturally want to justify ourselves and so struggle with the idea that salvation is one hundred per cent God's gift, entirely based on what Jesus has done and not at all based on what we do. Resistance to grace is not unique to Catholics; it's true of Muslims, Buddhists, Sikhs, Atheists and Agnostics, and far too often evangelical Christians too when our hearts forget what our heads know to be true.

CONTINUE ↓

Secondly, many Catholics have been told the reason people speak about salvation by grace alone is because they want to live sinful lives. I can remember as a young Christian trying to share the good news of Jesus with a Catholic I met on a Friday night. His response to me was "Your way is much easier, because you can live however you want." Though this argument might have been more powerful if he hadn't been drunk at the time, it is a frequent one. In a UK setting there's a common idea that the whole reason for the Protestant Reformation was simply so that Henry VIII could divorce Catherine of Aragon.

Suspicion that free grace leads to bad behaviour is older than the Tudors though; we find Saint Paul in the early verses of Romans 6 having to counter the idea that his gospel of grace meant that people would feel free to sin more and more.

YOU COULD TRY

So how might we talk to Catholic friends about this vitally important subject of being made right with God only through his grace? As with all the topics, we should look to ask questions, share Scripture and share our testimony, knowing we're not simply wanting to discuss the mechanics of theology but to point our friends to the risen Lord Jesus Christ, who is able "to save completely those who come to God through him" (Heb. 7:25).

We could ask the great diagnostic question, "If you were to stand before God today and he asked you, 'Why should I let you into my heaven?', what would you say?" But let's make sure we listen to our friend's answer, rather than just assuming we know what they will say before they open their mouth!

Depending on our friend's view of grace and works, we might ask questions such as "How many good works are enough to please God? Do you think you can ever be confident you've done enough?" Although these aren't comfortable questions to raise, they can lead to really fruitful conversations. Being honest about our own sinfulness and need of grace could really help Indifferent Ingrid see her own sin too, and we can go on to explain how wonderful it is that

Jesus lived the perfect life and freely gives that life to us when we trust him.

There are many parts of Scripture we can go to in order to talk directly about this subject, but one of my favourites is Ephesians 2:1-10, why not read it right now? God has raised us from death to life, saving us through faith, not by works, and so we can have a humble certainty of that salvation! What a joy this passage could be to Confused Connor, who has not yet recognised the joy of God's freely-given saving grace.

But as you look at these verses, don't forget verse 10, "For we are God's handiwork, created in Christ Jesus to do good works, which God prepared in advance for us to do." Doctrinal Danielle will need to hear that free grace doesn't lead to a sin-filled life, even as you show her Saint Paul is so clear that we do not do anything at any stage to contribute to our salvation. If we neglect to talk about that new life God calls us to, your Catholic friend may feel confirmed in their suspicion that evangelicals want to go on sinning, and all our talk about grace is simply an excuse for that.

GOOD TO KNOW:

If we are talking with Doctrinal Danny or Danielle about faith and works, it won't be long before James 2 comes up. You'll quickly be reminded that the only place in the Bible that the phrase "faith alone" occurs is James 2:24, which states, "You see that a person is considered righteous [or justified] by what they do and not by faith alone."

The recommended resources section includes an article that helps us understand James' words, but any good commentary will show that James is not protesting against Paul's message of grace through faith, rather he is teaching that a genuine trust in Christ will impact how we live. It's no good just claiming, "I trust in Jesus", and carrying on as before. This kind of "faith" cannot save, since it is a false, dead faith rather than a living faith.

Since the words of James are often set up in opposition to those of Paul, a good starting question to Danielle or Danny might be, "Because I think all of the Bible is God's Word, even if I can't fully explain it, I don't believe Saint James and Saint Paul are teaching opposite

CONTINUE ↓

things. Do you think Saint Paul got it wrong in Ephesians 2 when he said 'it is by grace you have been saved, through faith … not by works'?"

If your Catholic friend has been in any sense a regular churchgoer, they will almost certainly know about the dying thief to whom Jesus said "today you will be with me in paradise" (Lk. 23:43). If we remind them of this precious encounter, it is easy to ask what good works the thief was able to do after he entrusted himself to Christ and before dying. The answer is clear: none. And yet he was promised paradise by Christ himself!

And don't forget the opportunity for personal testimony, which can show our friend the reality of our relationship with God – ours by grace alone! I might say something like, "I love my children so much that I don't wait for them to earn the things I give them; I love to freely give them good gifts. And in coming to know Jesus, I found God to be far more like a loving Father than I had realised. Jesus reminds us that even imperfect, sinful fathers know how to give good gifts to their children. How much more God the Father loves to give good gifts to all who ask him! And the greatest gift of all is his own Son, who came to freely bring us back to God."

7

THE POPE
POWER AND AUTHORITY

A Christian once said to me, "We probably believe in a lot of the same things, but I don't believe the Pope is infallible." The great thing was, I – an active Catholic – didn't believe it either! The not-so-great thing was, it halted the conversation. Though it might be official Roman Catholic doctrine, as a baptised and active Catholic, I didn't believe in papal infallibility in any sense. That will be true of many of the Catholics you meet and want to engage in conversation.

However, the Catholic Church does teach that the Pope (meaning "Father", also known as the Bishop of Rome) has a unique authority to proclaim error-free truth about faith and morals – truth which must be held by all Christians. This is a huge claim, even when we understand that not everything the Pope says has infallible authority, but only those statements which are spoken *ex cathedra* ("from the seat").

GOOD TO KNOW:

The declaration of papal infallibility was made in "Pastor Aeternus", a document issued in 1870. Clearly, 1870 was a long, long way into the history of the church. However, as with many other doctrines, the claim is that this truth had always been held by the church. "Pastor Aeternus" contains a number of quotes from church history seeking to support the claim of the Pope's infallibility, although not all of these quotes seem relevant to this specific issue.

As well as considering tradition, Catholic teaching seeks to base its claims for the role and function of the Pope on Scripture. The key text is Matthew 16:13-19. Saint Peter has just confessed that Jesus is the promised Messiah, the Son of God. In response, Christ says,

> "Blessed are you, Simon son of Jonah, for this was not revealed to you by flesh and blood, but by my Father in heaven. And I tell you that you are Peter, and on this rock I will build my church, and the gates of Hades will not overcome it. I will give you the keys of the kingdom of heaven; whatever you bind on earth will be bound in heaven, and whatever you loose on earth will be loosed in heaven."

Here a Catholic and an evangelical can read the same words but, because of our prior assumptions, "hear" a totally different message. For the evangelical, the focus of this passage is very much on Christ being the promised Messiah who will spread the gospel and thus build his church through the apostles. For the Catholic (or at least for Danny and Danielle), the passage shows the unique status and authority of Saint Peter, the "rock" on which the church will be built, and implies that after Peter there will be others with the same role and authority as he had until Christ returns. Catholic teaching claims this is what is seen in church history; an unbroken succession of men who have sat in

Peter's seat as the Bishop of Rome and, with Peter's unique Christ-given authority, have ruled the church.

GOOD TO KNOW:

As an apostle of Christ, Peter had great authority which we should recognise. Matthew 16:19 tells us that Peter was given the keys of the kingdom of heaven, in order to bind and loose. However, just two chapters later, in Matthew 18:18 it is very clear that Jesus gives this same role to the whole group of apostles and not just Peter. All the apostles were to be involved in opening and closing the door of the kingdom of heaven as they shared the gospel and declared that those who turned to Christ were forgiven while those who rejected Christ remain bound in their sin.

While Peter's authority was not unique among the apostles, Scripture does suggest that the apostles themselves were unique. Unlike elders, the apostles were those who had seen the risen Christ and were able to authenticate the message about him. In his final letters (1 and 2 Timothy and Titus), Paul tells local churches

CONTINUE ↓

to appoint elders to govern in line with all the apostles and prophets had taught. Paul does not mention a successor to Peter as we would expect if Peter's role was ongoing.

LET'S BE HONEST

As we seek to talk with our Catholic friends about the gospel, Doctrinal Danny will likely insist that the Pope is God's representative – Christ's Vicar – on earth, and he is therefore the one all Christians must listen to. How can we address this subject? It is probably helpful to recognise that there have been "good", morally upright Popes in the history of the Catholic Church. Not all have been corrupt like Pope Alexander VI or Pope John XII (though obviously some have). We don't want to give the impression that we just think Popes are a bunch of meanies. Instead we believe that the role of Supreme Pontiff of the Universal Church is not a valid one for even the godliest person.

It is also helpful to confess to ourselves, and to Catholic friends, that there have been evangelical pastors who have overplayed their authority in ungodly ways. If we give the impression that we think Protestants have a perfect record of godly leadership, our valid critique of the role of an infallible Pope will lose all force; it will seem that we are trying to remove a speck from our Catholic neighbour's eye while ignoring the log in our own. This approach might be one way to engage Indifferent Ingrid, who may recognise that spiritual power is often abused. If we are willing to recognise this abuse within our own setting, we can then point with greater reality to Christ's perfect, loving authority.

YOU COULD TRY

You could ask Doctrinal Danny or Danielle, "If Saint Peter is *the* rock, does it follow that today's Pope is the head of the universal church?" As well as looking together at Matthew 18:18 where all the disciples are given the same authority, you could read Acts 15 where Peter is just one among the speakers at the Jerusalem Council, and even Galatians 2:11-21 where Paul corrects Peter. You could ask whether the special authority of Saint Peter was unique among the apostles, and whether it was an authority that was meant to be passed down through the generations.

You could also say, "We don't agree about whether there is a succession of men directly taking on Saint Peter's role. However, we do both agree that Saint Peter had an awesome Christ-given authority to proclaim God's Word. Would you like to look at his letters together, or at a couple of his sermons in the book of Acts?" After all, these do have an unending authority. As you read, ask questions. Don't feel that you need to be constantly pushing against Catholic doctrine, especially if you are talking with Confused Connor who may not even be aware of that doctrine; just enjoy looking at God's Word with a friend.

Why not ask your friend if they can tell you what they find helpful about the idea of an infallible Pope? Born-Again Bobby may gain a sense of security in a changing and unstable world, from having an infallible leader who is also a loving "Papa". This seeming stability may also attract people – including evangelicals – to the Church of Rome. The reality though is often far different.

Despite institutional "unity" under the leadership of the Pope, true unity is just as ethereal in Rome as it is in Protestantism, with very different views on the gospel and Christ's kingdom being held by different Catholics.[1] Even different Popes within my lifetime have, at the very least, had markedly different emphases, with some more traditional and others more progressive. In practice an infallible Pope does not give the sure and steady foundation you would hope for from a solid rock and so we desire our Catholic friend to find security not in an infallible leader (either religious or political), but in the Son of God.

The Lord Jesus is the One with all authority in heaven and on earth (Mt. 28:18). He is utterly unfailing and unchanging, lives in us by his Spirit, and will in the end bring all his people to true unity. Is there an episode in your life when you really had to lean on the Lord Jesus in the midst of very tough times? Could you tell that story to your Catholic friend, pointing them to the utterly trustworthy Rock who never fails?

8
MARY
SAINT AND SINNER

"Who do you say I am?" is a question Jesus famously asked his disciples during his ministry. It was an incredibly important question to which Saint Peter was able to reply with the wonderful truth that Jesus is God's Son, the Messiah (Mt. 16:16).

However, let's place that same question in the mouth of Jesus' mother Mary, "Who do you say I am?" Eddie Evangelical may reply, "Mary is the mother of Jesus but she's a sinner, like the rest of us." Our Catholic friend might answer, "Mary is the Mother of God, Queen of Heaven and Earth, and the Mediatrix of all graces." These are very different views! Let's consider why a Catholic might answer in this way.

SINLESS AND ASSUMED?

The Catholic Church has a much higher view of Mary than evangelicals do; let's look briefly at two dogmas (binding doctrines) which demonstrate the status Mary is given in official Catholic teaching.

Firstly, in 1854 Pope Pius IX defined the dogma of the Immaculate Conception, meaning Mary was conceived without sin, and that she remained without sin throughout life. (Though she did not need saving from sin's consequences, the Catholic Church can still speak of God saving Mary from sin, since in its view she was saved from having a sinful nature and from committing sin.)

Secondly, Pope Pius XII said in 1950, "We pronounce, declare, and define it to be a divinely revealed dogma: that the Immaculate Mother of God, the ever Virgin Mary, having completed the course of her earthly life, was assumed body and soul into heavenly glory."[1] Other believers die and their soul goes to be with the Lord in heaven while their body remains on earth. Mary, however, not only died but her body was raised again along with her soul before she went to heaven.

These two dogmas place Mary alongside the Lord Jesus in ways which can easily undermine his uniqueness. Was Jesus born without sin, and did he continue throughout life without sin? This is true of Mary as well, according to Catholic dogma. Doesn't Jesus have a resurrected body now in heaven, whereas others must wait till the second coming until their body is raised? Yes, but so does his mother, formal Catholic teaching states. As dogmas of the Catholic Church, Mary's sinlessness and assumption into heaven cannot be rejected by any faithful Catholic. At least, that is the theory. You've probably guessed that the beliefs of individual Catholics about Mary are just as diverse as they are on any other topic.

Although Mary's sinlessness and bodily assumption cannot be founded on what the Scriptures plainly say, this doesn't challenge a traditional Catholic in the way it would an evangelical. Informed Catholics like Danny and Danielle are able to find a developing doctrine of Mary through the history of the church and, for them, that tradition holds the same authority as a direct statement of Scripture.

GOOD TO KNOW:

Mary's lifelong virginity is also a Catholic dogma. Of course, all evangelicals believe that Mary was a virgin when the Holy Spirit overshadowed her and the Lord Jesus began to grow in her womb. It is also universally understood that she remained a virgin until after the birth of Jesus. However, it might surprise you that many Protestants, including some of the Reformers, have held to the perpetual virginity of Mary. Though verses such as Matthew 1:18, Matthew 1:25 and Mark 3:31 cause me to think that after Jesus' birth, Mary and Joseph enjoyed a "normal" marriage, the doctrine of perpetual virginity is not harmful to the gospel in the same way the other two dogmas are.

YOU COULD TRY

The claim to Mary's sinlessness is one I find more common with Catholic friends than her being raised bodily to heaven, so let's focus on that. Here are two possible approaches:

Approach 1: "You're a Catholic – so you believe that Mary was sinless even though the Bible says everyone is a sinner?" Of course Romans 3:23 clearly teaches that all have sinned and fallen short of God's glory. However, there are two big problems with this approach.

Firstly, this is likely to come across as insulting to someone who (too-highly) values Mary – it may well sound a lot like a "your momma" joke and be immediately off-putting to your friend. In fact, just as people may be happy to criticise their own parents but be very offended if someone else does, even Indifferent Ingrid, though happy to criticise Catholic belief, may have a similar emotional reaction if you seem to criticise "Mother Mary" to her.

Secondly, by asking this question, you have simply assumed your friend holds the formal Catholic teaching about Mary. Confused Connor or Born-Again Bobby may not even believe that teaching, so you may be aiming wide of the target.

Approach 2: "What do you think about Mary? I love her song 'The Magnificat' in the first chapter of Saint Luke's Gospel. Shall we have a look at it together?" I would recommend this approach with any Catholic friend. As you open up Luke 1:46-55, you will discover all kinds of wonderful truths that Mary, the servant of the Lord, expressed about God.

You don't need to rush to do so, but as you explore together, you can gently ask, "When Mary describes God as her Saviour in verse 47, what do you think she meant? What do you think she needed to be saved from? Do you think when she speaks about his mercy in verse 50 she knew *she* needed that mercy?" Here, we are taking the words of Mary herself seriously; surely anyone with a high view of Mary will want to do that.

TO CONSIDER:

The Catholic answer to Mary's "Who do you say I am?" is too high, but Eddie Evangelical's answer is too limited. Mary was a sinner. But she also had a unique part to play in God's plan of salvation. We should ensure we don't downplay this, or we can risk looking like we are insulting the mother of our Lord. We need to think not only about what we are saying to our Catholic

CONTINUE ↓

friends, but also try to consider what they are hearing. We shouldn't say more about Mary than the Bible says. But we should feel able to say everything about Mary that the Scriptures teach.

DEVOTION TO MARY

In addition to formal Catholic teaching, you may discover your Catholic friend has a very Mary-centric devotional life. Though my personal Marian devotion didn't go beyond occasionally saying the Hail Mary – a prayer addressed to Mary herself – for many Catholics devotion to Mary is huge. The Rosary is one example among many of this. These prayer beads regularly used by many devout Catholics contain a total of fifty-nine beads, each representing a prayer. Of these prayers, the vast majority are addressed to Mary.

While it is true that official Catholic teaching does not allow worship to anyone other than God the Father, Son and Holy Spirit, it is understandable that evangelicals see praying more to Mary than to God as constituting a form of idolatry. Though we should rightly denounce this idolatry, we want to understand our friend's thinking, and help them understand more of what the Scriptures teach. So let's consider: Why would speaking to Mary more than to God himself be popular for many Catholics?

Perhaps the mindset can be understood by looking at this prayer, addressed to Mary:

> "O Mother of Perpetual Help ... if thou protect me, dear Mother, I fear nothing; not from my sins, because thou wilt obtain for me the pardon of them; nor from the devils, because thou art more powerful than all hell together; nor even from Jesus, my Judge himself, because by one prayer from thee he will be appeased."[2]

While informed Catholics recognise that this prayer may be unhelpful, it certainly reflects the thinking of many Catholics. In Mary, they believe they find someone who has the ear of her son Jesus, but who is more compassionate.

Of course, we can point to the fact that God has given us *one* Mediator, Christ Jesus (1 Tim. 2:5), and so we do not need Mary, or any of the other Saints, to go to God for us. This can certainly be helpful. But if I am in deadly fear of Jesus, and think he is waiting to strike me down in his wrath, I am unlikely to come to him, even if I know there is nobody else to come to. So why not also take your Catholic friend to one or more of the many Gospel narratives which show that they will find in Jesus the wonderful compassion they may have been seeking in Mary.

Perhaps go to a passage such as Luke 7:11-17, where we see Jesus helping a hopeless widow who has just lost her son. Why not carry on in the same chapter to see how Jesus not only forgave but also honoured a woman who had previously lived a sinful life. She found in Jesus the compassion denied to her everywhere else (vv36-50). Isn't this the mediator we all want? Isn't he more wonderful, compassionate, and full of pity, than anyone else?

TO CONSIDER:

Of course, "Who do you say I am?" is not a question we see Mary ask in the Scriptures. We see the Lord Jesus asking that question. If we spend all our time speaking with our Catholic friends about Mary, we are not doing them any favours. In overly putting the spotlight on Mary,

CONTINUE ↓

even in a corrective sense, we are not doing what Mary would want us to be doing. Rather, by helping our friends see Jesus more clearly, we are doing something that will be hugely beneficial for them – perhaps eternally so. Let's make sure we don't cause a stumbling block through the way we speak about Mary, when we want to point our friends to her Son!

9

COMMUNION

TAKE AND EAT

Even as I began to realise my Catholic Church did not embrace some important aspects of biblical truth, I became very aware of something else. Other churches could not offer me what the Catholic Church did: Christ's true body and blood in Communion. If what I had been taught growing up was correct, then surely the Catholic Mass (alternatively known as Communion, the Eucharist or the Lord's Supper) was the "source and summit of the Christian life".[1] As I wrestled with this in my late teens, I felt I couldn't leave the Catholic Church if it alone had the most important thing of all – the only thing that can bring me forgiveness and bring me home.

This is a deep subject, with many hundreds of years of thought and reflection behind it, so as we seek to share the gospel with our Catholic friend, let's do so humbly. A helpful starting place might be to recognise that Protestants have historically been (and remain) divided on this issue. Indeed, Protestantism's first major division came in 1529 when Luther and Zwingli (a Reformer from Zurich, Switzerland) could not agree on the nature of the Lord's Supper. We don't need to master all the theological arguments and debates before we talk to a Catholic friend about communion, but we will greatly help our conversation if we discuss this issue graciously, admitting evangelicals don't always agree, and understanding how important it may be to them.

GOOD TO KNOW:

The Catechism of the Catholic Church gives over twenty-two pages to "The Sacrament of the Eucharist", and there is much to enjoy. The

CONTINUE ↓

authors tie the Last Supper back to the Passover and the Israelites' release from slavery in Egypt, and point the reader forward, reminding us that the bread and wine we share is "also an anticipation of the heavenly glory".[2]

However, the Catechism is also very clear that in the Mass, the bread and wine, while retaining the same appearance, actually become – through the work of God – the literal body and blood of Christ, even as he remains seated in heaven.[3] This is known as transubstantiation. To claim otherwise is, to the Roman Catholic Church, a deadly error. The Council of Trent in the sixteenth century said, "If anyone denies, that, in the sacrament of the most holy Eucharist, are contained truly, really, and substantially, the body and blood together with the soul and divinity of our Lord Jesus Christ, and consequentially the whole Christ; but saith that He is only therein as in a sign, or a figure, or a virtue; let him be anathema."[4] This cuts off from the church (and quite possibly from salvation) Protestants holding to a range of other views on the Lord's Supper.

WHY DOES IT MATTER?

As with every topic discussed in this book, we can't assume every Catholic will believe and value the same thing, so – you guessed it – if the subject comes up, ask your friend what the Mass means to them, rather than assume you know what they think!

As a young Catholic, I strongly believed that the bread and wine became the body and blood of Christ. Week by week, I believed I was literally taking and eating his body, and taking and drinking his blood – as he had commanded. While I look back and recognise that I was wrong, I also see that I was seeking to take the words of the Lord Jesus, "this is my body" (Mt. 26:26), seriously in the way I had been taught.

TO CONSIDER:

It's right to encourage our Catholic friends to come to a church where they will hear the Bible clearly taught and we should pray the Lord will help them see how good it would be to be part of an evangelical church. But we need to recognise there might be lots of reasons why even Born-

CONTINUE ↓

Again Bobby might resist leaving the Catholic Church, not least the issue of Communion. Patience, love and understanding will be hugely valuable to our friend, even if they end up continuing on in a Catholic Church until the end of their life.

Believing the bread and wine become the actual body and blood of Christ may be one of the barriers stopping your Catholic friend going to a more biblically based church, as it was for me. But whether we're chatting to a Born-Again Bobby, Confused Connor or Doctrinal Danny, there are better and worse ways to approach the subject.

APPROACHES TO AVOID

Here's the worst approach that, sadly, I have encountered from evangelical believers both at school and at theological college: "How on earth could anyone think the bread and wine are Jesus' body and blood? Just look at them! Just taste them! How can anyone be gullible enough to think they've transformed?" As popular as mockery can be – especially online – it is of course much more likely to alienate than convince a Catholic friend.

Others have tried the argument "If it looks like a dog, walks like a dog and barks like a dog then it must be a dog" to seek to convince a Catholic that the bread and wine remains just that; all our senses tell us it remains the same. This approach might be helpful to an Indifferent Ingrid who hasn't really thought about the topic. However, if your friend is convinced that Jesus' teaching should be given more weight than seemingly-logical arguments, there's something commendable about that! We want them to listen to Jesus more than to us. How can we help them do that?

YOU COULD TRY

I'd suggest the best way to engage with our Catholic friend is to help them see that Jesus himself wasn't claiming the bread and wine as his literal body and blood. So, we might rightly point out that Jesus also said, "I am the gate" (Jn. 10:9); "I am the vine" (Jn. 15:5); and so on. You might say, "Do you remember when Jesus said 'I am the gate' – we'd agree that he didn't mean that literally. He was saying that he was the way for us to come to God. When Jesus said, 'I am the bread of life' (Jn. 6:35), what do you think he meant there? And when he said, 'This is my body given for you' (Lk. 22:19), have you considered that he might have meant something figurative there too?"

You may then have opportunity to explain to your friend that when Jesus said he is the bread of life, he was saying he is the one who feeds and nourishes us. When he said "this is my body", he was giving us a meal by which we could remember all he achieved for us at the cross, and through which he would spiritually strengthen us.

It can also be helpful to go to a passage like 1 Corinthians 11, where Saint Paul speaks of eating the bread and drinking the cup (v26) which Christ has referred to as his body and blood (vv24-25). Why did Paul speak of eating the bread if it is no longer bread, but has become the body of Christ?

Finally, you should seek to value the Lord's Supper. Whatever view you take on it, ensure that you are seeking to be built up in Christ by it. Then, be willing and unembarrassed to speak warmly of how you meet with the Lord as you eat and drink.

John H. Armstrong, who edited *Understanding Four Views on the Lord's Supper* says in his conclusion to the book, "the most important point is to *commune* as [Christ] taught us, not simply to *debate* the meaning of Communion".[5] We don't do the souls of our Catholic friends, or our own souls, much good by being constantly in debate mode. Let's ensure as we consider this important subject that we remember what it points to and delight in the Saviour whose body was broken to make us whole and whose blood flowed to wash us clean. As we do so, may our faces shine out to others with the glory of communion with Christ.

10

PURGATORY

DEATH AND BEYOND

"As soon as the coin in the coffer rings,
the soul from purgatory springs."

These famous words were spoken by Johann Tetzel, a sixteenth-century friar in Germany. He was encouraging people to buy *indulgences*, which would enable them to release their loved ones from the sufferings of purgatory and speed their way to heaven. A young monk named Martin Luther heard that this was happening in a nearby town. Concerned about the pastoral implications to his people, he decided to write down and publish a number of objections against the abusive practice of selling indulgences – ninety-five of them, in fact!

Purgatory, and particularly the abuses that surrounded teaching on it, was an important catalyst to the Protestant Reformation. It might seem surprising, then, that less than one page is directly devoted to the doctrine in the 600-page *Catechism of the Catholic Church*.

WHAT IS PURGATORY?

Purgatory is described in this way, "All who die in God's grace and friendship, but still imperfectly purified, are indeed assured of their eternal salvation; but after death they undergo purification, so as to achieve the holiness necessary to enter the joy of heaven."[1]

According to Catholic doctrine, purgatory is a place where believers go after death, in order to be made perfectly pure before entering God's immediate presence. Importantly, it is not a place for unbelievers, but only those "who die in God's grace and friendship".[2] This purification is a form of punishment, though not an eternal one and not directly from God.[3]

TO CONSIDER:

Doctrinal Danny or Danielle might say, "Surely you recognise that when you die, you will be far from perfect? That is why purgatory is necessary for most of us; it is the place we go in order to be made perfect, fit for the presence of God." There is a seeming logic to this. But is it in line with the gospel?

We could open up 2 Corinthians with a friend who thinks this way, and see that Saint Paul talks about the time between death and Jesus' return very differently. He looks forward to this time when we will be in heaven "away from the body and at home with the Lord" (2 Cor. 5:8).

The doctrine of purgatory very much stands or falls with what Jesus Christ achieved on the cross. It relates very closely to our understanding of how we are justified before God.

The Catholic teaching that Christ dealt with the *eternal* punishment of our sin on the cross, but that there is still a *temporal* punishment to be dealt with in purgatory, robs believers of assurance. It can cause them to live all their lives held in slavery to the fear of death – in contrast to evangelical teaching that Jesus dealt with all punishment so we can go straight to heaven when we die (Heb. 2:14-15).

GOOD TO KNOW:

The truth that Christ's death once for all (Heb. 7:27) frees us from sin's eternal *and* temporal punishment is the good news of the gospel. This is the very thing that separates Christianity from every other religion and worldview. While other religions teach us that we must *do* in order to receive divine favour, the Bible tells us that God has loved and favoured us in spite of our sin, and that he has already *done* everything to forgive us and bring us home.

Of course, God does work in us to gradually purify us from sin throughout this life, and this purification will not be complete by the time we die. But Christians can be confident that "to die is gain", and we can look forward to the day we "depart and be with Christ, which is better by far" (Phil. 1:21-23). Immediately when we die, we will be made sinless and go to heaven. Our final purification is not based on an indefinite time that we will spend suffering in purgatory, but based on what he has already achieved for us through his suffering. It is worth pointing out to our Catholic friend that this does not lead to a carelessness about holiness, but is rather a great motivation to purify ourselves (1 Jn. 3:3).

GOOD TO KNOW:

Of course, Catholic teaching does marshal church history and Scripture to attempt to show the legitimacy of purgatory. The clearest passage that a Catholic can turn to is 2 Maccabees 12:39-45, which is included in the Catholic Deuterocanon. There we find the Jewish warrior Judas Maccabeus making prayers and an offering for members of his army who had died wearing idolatrous "tokens" (probably jewellery of some kind). Though I do not consider it Scripture, if Doctrinal Danny or Danielle were to raise this passage, I might ask, "Do you think the sin of idolatry can be forgiven without repentance?" (Catholic teaching says

CONTINUE ↓

that it cannot be.) Since, in Catholic teaching, these men remain unforgiven, they did not die in God's grace and friendship and so would go to hell rather than purgatory. The prayers of Judas Maccabeus therefore would have done nothing to help them.

Another verse Danny or Danielle might appeal to in support of purgatory is 1 Corinthians 3:10-15, which speaks of a person being saved "though only as one escaping through the flames". When looked at in context it's clear that Paul is teaching about heavenly rewards and not purgatory. If this passage comes up, why not read it together with your friend and ask, "When will all this happen according to verse 13?" Paul is talking about the quality of our Christian service being "tested" and "shown for what it is" on the final Judgment Day, rather than any sort of purifying process before this time. The good news is that even those whose work "is burned up … will [still] be saved".

YOU COULD TRY

Here's the last time you'll hear me say this, I promise, but of course your Catholic friend might not believe in purgatory at all, or their view of it might be very different to the official view. How can we helpfully talk with our Catholic friend about eternity, in a way that points them to the certain hope of Jesus?

Rather than asking in an accusatory way, "Why do you believe in purgatory when the Bible doesn't even talk about it?", why not find out if they do believe in it? As we've seen, they might not! How about this question instead, "What do you think happens after we die? Are you confident of heaven? Why?" This could lead to a fruitful conversation with Confused Connor, who perhaps is uncertain about what happens when we die or how we can attain heaven.

With this question, we are straight into talking about how Christ's work on the cross fully deals with sin and the meaning of his words "It is finished" as he drew his last breath (Jn. 19:30). We could also talk about the end of Hebrews 9 and through chapter 10 showing that, gloriously, there is no need for purgatory. We can tell our friend that if they turn from sin and trust in Christ, they will be delivered from hell because of what he has done, and are on their way to heaven. Isn't it wonderful to be able to say on the authority of God's Word that all who die in the Lord go straight to be with him!

We could also ask, "What are you looking forward to about heaven?" This is a good question to think through for ourselves as well. We might hope Born-Again Bobby will be delighted to speak about the joys of eternity with us and we'll be encouraged as she does so.

And whatever the response, we can point to Revelation 21:1-7 which shows us that in the New Creation there is no suffering or sadness. There is a hunger in all of us for this future – even Indifferent Ingrid can feel that longing, and we can talk with her about how our trust in Christ gives us a hope for a better future and strength to work for love and justice today. Revelation 21 also tells us there will be no sin – our friend who struggles with whether they are good enough for God will be pleased to hear that. Most of all, the Lord will be with his people in heaven. All who trust in Christ will be there with him!

CONCLUSION

THE WAY AHEAD

Thank you for getting right to the end! Now you've read this book does that mean that, at long last, you are equipped to share the good news with a Catholic?

No.

You had all you needed before you began!

Throughout this book, I hope I've given you some guidance in sensitively sharing truths about Christ with individual Catholic friends. But if you are a Christian, you were *already* able to share the gospel with a Catholic friend before you began reading. Knowing the gospel of Jesus Christ, and having his Spirit in you giving you a desire to live for the Father, qualifies you to share your faith with *anyone*!

The real focus of this book hasn't been on understanding Roman Catholic doctrine so much as on understanding your Catholic friends. You may wish to read or listen to other resources to more deeply understand what your friend believes and what makes them tick. You might want to consider some other important areas of Catholic doctrine such as the nature of the church, how the church holds and dispenses God's grace through its sacraments such as baptism and confession, the relationship of other religions to God's saving grace, and many more.

In all this, it's crucial to recognise that it's far more worthwhile to concentrate on important gospel issues than on obvious but non-essential differences, such as how the minister dresses. But whatever the topic of conversation and whether it's Danny or Danielle, Connor, Ingrid or Bobby, you are already equipped by the Holy Spirit to share the glorious good news of the Father's free salvation through his Son.

So as you share this gospel with friends, let me encourage you with the words of the benediction I heard for years at the end of every Catholic Mass I attended, "Go in peace to love and serve the Lord."

RECOMMENDED RESOURCES

Two YouTube channels that deal well with Roman Catholic doctrine (among other topics) are Gavin Ortlund's "Truth Unites" and Dr. Jordan B. Cooper's "Just & Sinner". Their output is fair, thorough and gracious.

A simple online article by R.C. Sproul to help you understand James 2 is "Does James 2:24 Deny Justification by Faith Alone?" and can be found at Ligonier.org.

You'll also find more that I've written on these issues on my blog "Not That Richard Baxter", where I have a section specifically on Catholic resources. My blog can be found here:

There are many helpful books available on Roman Catholicism. I particularly recommend:

A Christian's Pocket Guide to the Papacy by Leonardo de Chirico (Christian Focus, 2015). Leonardo is an evangelical pastor who is also an expert on modern Roman Catholicism. This helpful guide will give further background to how the role of the Pope has developed over the centuries, and why it is problematic. He also has a similar short guide on Mary in the same series.

Roman Catholic Theology and Practice by Gregg R. Allison (Crossway, 2014). This chunky book is a great resource if you are friends with Doctrinal Danny or Danielle and really want to understand points of similarity and difference between official Catholic teaching and evangelical teaching.

Talking with Catholics about the Gospel by Chris Castaldo (Zondervan, 2015). Chris's love for Catholics shines through in all his work. In this book he is able to spend longer on doctrinal beliefs and their historical shaping than I have been able to here.

Finally a great book to give away to a Catholic friend is:

Nothing in My Hand I Bring by Ray Galea (Matthias Media, 2007). Because of the wide range of "Catholic" thinking and beliefs, I'm not convinced there could be one resource which is suitable for every Catholic we encounter. However, if I were to give one piece of literature (other than the Bible) to a self-consciously Catholic friend, I think this might be it.

ENDNOTES

CHAPTER 1

1 Peter Kreeft, *Reclaiming the Great Tradition* (IVP, 1997), p. 27.

CHAPTER 5

1 *Catechism of the Catholic Church* (Geoffrey Chapman, 1994), para. 82.

CHAPTER 6

1 "On Justification, Canon I", General Council of Trent: Sixth Session (1547), https://www.papalencyclicals.net/councils/trent/sixth-session.htm

2 *Catechism of the Catholic Church*, para. 2027.

3 "On Justification, Canon IX", General Council of Trent: Sixth Session.

CHAPTER 7

1 See, for example, the tensions acknowledged by a well-known Catholic apologist: Trent Horn, "Liberal

Catholics? Conservative Catholics?" *Catholic Answers Magazine* (8/12/2024), https://www.catholic.com/magazine/online-edition/liberal-catholics-conservative-catholics

CHAPTER 8

1 Pope Pius XII, "Munificentissimus Deus: Defining the Dogma of the Assumption" (1950), https://www.papalencyclicals.net/pius12/p12munif.htm

2 "Our Mother of Perpetual Help Devotions", Daily Catholic, https://www.dailycatholic.org/perpetua.htm

CHAPTER 9

1 *Catechism of the Catholic Church*, para. 1324.

2 *Catechism of the Catholic Church*, para. 1402.

3 *Catechism of the Catholic Church*, para. 1413.

4 "On the Most Holy Sacrament of the Eucharist, Canon IX", General Council of Trent: Thirteenth Session (1551), https://www.papalencyclicals.net/councils/trent/thirteenth-session.htm

5 John H. Armstrong, *Understanding Four Views on the Lord's Supper* (Zondervan, 2007), pp. 154-5.

CHAPTER 10

1 *Catechism of the Catholic Church*, para. 1030.

2 *Catechism of the Catholic Church*, para. 1030.

3 *Catechism of the Catholic Church*, para. 1472.